MEANING AND PURPOSE IN
THE SECOND HALF OF LIFE

MEANING AND PURPOSE IN THE SECOND HALF OF LIFE

A Guide to Finding What to Do with the Rest of Your Life

Next Avenue

ISBN-13: 978-1-62764-015-2
ISBN-10: 1627640150

TABLE OF CONTENTS

INTRODUCTION

People often find themselves at a crossroads in their 50s and 60s. Their professional path may no longer be as rewarding or as full of options as it once was, they may be facing an empty nest, or their significant relationships may be shifting ground. For many, the only thing that's clear is the question "Now what?"

With the possibility of 30 or more years of life ahead, those in midlife often find themselves yearning to abandon or overhaul past approaches and set fresh, positive ones in motion.

This stage of life is actually the perfect time to reinvent — or reawaken — the most authentic and meaningful parts of ourselves. Relieved of many of our previous commitments, we are free to probe the measure of our own experience and wisdom and pursue things that can make our hearts and souls sing.

This e-book gathers advice and wisdom from blogs and articles written for nextavenue.org, a web site designed for those in this new phase of life that we call Adult, Part 2. Next Avenue is for grown-ups who want to keep growing, learning and evolving. We offer these insights for discovering fresh perspective and meaning, delving into invigorating pursuits, and sparking a renewed sense of purpose.

WHAT WILL YOU DO WITH THE REST OF YOUR LIFE?

Gleaning inspiration and wisdom from elderly role models can show us how to make the most of our bonus years

By Donna Sapolin

Donna Sapolin, the founding Vice President and Editorial Director of Next Avenue, is a multi-platform media consultant, editor and writer who has led many leading magazines and websites and written hundreds of articles.

I recently became a member of a small local gym. However, despite my good intentions, almost immediately after joining, I found myself making excuses for why I couldn't do this or that exercise. Most of my excuses had to do with my bad knees.

After a few weeks of very limited use, I could see a chain reaction in the making. If I let simple aches stop me now, I reasoned, it wouldn't be long before I'd have an excuse for avoiding pretty much anything that can keep me active, vibrant, learning and contributing.

Enough excuse making, I chided myself while watching a huge group of seniors practice dance-like t'ai chi movements in Central Park this past weekend. I resolved that I'd look into this ancient Chinese martial art, as well as yoga, whose popularity has continued to explode.

I read up on the enormous health benefits each of these practices confers and decided I should sign up for a yoga class, either at my new gym (though they offer only one class a week) or elsewhere, but one led by an instructor who can help modify the positions so that my knee problems don't interfere.

A Revered Yogi

While doing this research, I learned about an amazing 94-year-old woman, Tao Porchon-Lynch, who has been practicing yoga for more than 70 years and teaching it for 45, while also doing competitive ballroom dancing and sustaining a robust speaking schedule — and all this despite a hip replacement a few years ago.

She's the founder of the Westchester Institute of Yoga in Hartsdale, N.Y., and over the years has taught more than 400 students, whom she calls her children. A year ago, she was designated "The World's Oldest Yoga Teacher" by the Guinness Book of World Records.

As I watched Porchon-Lynch demonstrate yoga poses that many people a third of her age would find difficult, if not impossible, to hold, I could see that she embodies the principle emblazoned on every page of her website: "There is Nothing You Cannot Do."

Over the years, Porchon-Lynch has been asked by many to share her ideas regarding her longevity and purpose. In an interview last October with Julie Bryant of Naked Dragon, she urged people not to procrastinate. "If you do something you believe in, it may not turn out exactly the way you think," she said, "but it's usually better than what you wanted."

She also emphasized the importance of continuing to learn on a daily basis. "Every day, the dawn of life starts again," she said. "I live better each day."

When Bryant comments on Porcon-Lynch's sparkling eyes, the yoga teacher says that they're just mirroring back what she sees in her students.

The incredible motivation and inspiration she provides to others have brought to mind some other remarkable elders with whom I spent time during my early career as a writer — women and men whose youthful appearance, activities and zest for living belied their age. Each left an indelible impression and, at the time, helped me formulate a personal prescription for aging well. It now seems worthwhile to summon up those long-buried memories and remind myself of that prescription.

A Legendary Potter

I interviewed the renowned potter Beatrice Wood when she was 101 years old. (She died at 104.) She had eaten a vegetarian diet since the age of 17, lived in the spectacular hills above Ojai, California, surrounded by loving companions, and spent her mornings making lustrous pottery. Decked out in a glorious silk sari, with silver bangles stacked high along her arm, I recall her swooning when a handsome, young man walked into the front hall of her house-gallery. "Hold on!," she said, interrupting our discussion. "I'm in love."

When she wasn't making pottery, Wood surrounded herself with visitors of all ages and held court. At the time we met, she was almost deaf but that didn't stop her from leaning in closely, following my lip movements and telling riveting tales about her life and work. Her sense of delight was evident throughout.

A Renowned Chef

I saw the same vibrant spirit and work ethic in Julia Child, who was a columnist for Food & Wine magazine when I worked there. I once sat across from her at a dinner party and watched her shower attention on everyone around her. She was 82 and had recently lost the love of her life, her husband, Paul Child. Her gracious interactions and open heart showed us all how to fill the gaping hole that opens after a great love exits.

Not long after, I attended a taping of an episode of her popular PBS TV show, *Cooking with Master Chefs,* in Jacques Pepin's recently renovated kitchen, which I would be writing about. After many hours of shooting, we took a break and, as others headed outside to chat and stretch, Child took a few halting steps over to a small café table in the corner where she promptly began typing on a laptop. She saw me looking at her with a questioning expression, smiled and explained that she needed to make progress on a new book project.

A Soulful Woodworker

George Nakashima greeted me in his Pennsylvania woodworking workshop not long after he had written a book called *The Soul of a Tree.* He was in his mid-eighties. Though more reserved than the female creators I had met, this masterful carver of furniture described his deep and invigorating connection to nature and wood.

During World War II, he and his family were uprooted and moved to an internment camp, where he learned about traditional Japanese hand tools from a fellow prisoner, a carpenter.

After telling me about this experience and emphasizing the lessons rather than the hardships, he quickly moved on to his philosophy regarding craftsmanship, design and his life's mission. The site that's dedicated to his legacy and the studio his daughter now runs expresses it very much the way he did: "Our approach is based on direct experience — a way of life and development outward from an inner core; something of the same process that nature uses in the creation of a tree — with one addition, the aspiration of man to produce the wonder and beauty of his potentialities."

Nakashima, who worked until the day he died in 1990 and whose stunning works are collected the world over, was without question devoted to expressing "the wonder and beauty of his potentialities."

While many of us are going to live a longer, more active life than previous generations due to medical advancements, we can't assume that extra years will bring greater wisdom or the will to be productive. Wisdom, as we've often heard, is something one earns. To grow, we have to commit ourselves to various types of experiences and to gleaning their lessons, both overt and hidden. What gives us the will to keep going is, I believe, a matter of having good reasons to do so. But, as the elders I describe suggest, it's on us to find and shape the reasons.

Continuing to stay actively engaged in something you love, mentoring others and interacting with people are the well-established keys to aging well, as exemplified by the elders I've cited. While each had infirmities and endured huge obstacles, they adapted to their circumstances and didn't make excuses. They did everything in their power to overcome their hurdles and renew their sense of purpose.

Another powerful example of such persistence was captured in a recent New York Times article, "A Writing Coach Becomes a Listener." It profiles a 91-year-old writer who can no longer see yet continues to teach his craft to students by listening to their written words.

Legacies to Learn From

Those who perhaps haven't always lived to the fullest can provide additional insight into making not only the bonus years but all of life more meaningful. Karl Pillemer, a Cornell psychologist and founder of the Legacy Project, has made sharing the wisdom of elders his focus. According to the project's site, it "has systematically collected practical advice from over 1,500 older Americans who have lived through extraordinary experiences and historical events. They offer tips on surviving and thriving despite the challenges we all encounter."

It's well worth combing through the many categories the site addresses; Next Avenue delivered some career advice from some of the wise people Pillemer interviewed. These tips include saying "yes" to career opportunities even if you fear that you are unqualified, being willing to take a pay cut if the job will make you happy, making the most of a job you dislike by turning it into a learning experience, expressing interest in others and staying even-keeled on the job, and opting for work that gives you as much personal freedom as possible.

Given the likelihood of a longer life, we owe it to ourselves to figure out how to make it worthwhile. Fortunately, there's a lot of inspiration out there waiting to be discovered. We need only look.

5 ABILITIES YOU NEED TO MASTER AFTER 50

Boomers who learn these abilities are likely to flourish both personally and professionally

By George H. Schofield

George H. Schofield, Ph.D., is a business consultant, speaker and professor, specializing in organizational psychology and career development. He is a former vice president for the Bank of America, a board member of several nonprofits and author of 'After 50 It's Up to Us: Developing the Skills and Agility We'll Need.'

In 1976, when my father was 60, he and his peers held a fairly optimistic view of later life.

They had survived the Depression and two world wars; they would retire with modest pensions; their mortgages were paid off, so they could live in their homes at low cost for a long time; their children were grown, had good jobs and families of their own. Finally, there was plenty of time for hobbies and fun.

In 2013, many of my boomer peers hold a very different view of later life. Our future is less predictable and those golden years sometimes seem more like tarnished brass.

Instead of coasting into our 70s and 80s, we face interruption unimagined by our elders: discontinued income streams; increasing rates of later-in-life divorce and bankruptcy; the potential for sharp declines in the value of our retirement portfolio and property.

What Boomers Will Encounter

Although boomers are not a homogenous group culturally, politically or spiritually, nearly all of us can count on three things in the future:

* Interruptions in our lives will persist.

* Our capacity for flexibility and adaptability will determine quality of life.

* Many of us will live significantly longer, healthier lives than once expected, which means we'll need appropriate financial resources to make them worthwhile.

The 5 Key Abilities to Flourish

Under these circumstances, there are five key abilities boomers will need to flourish:

1. **Identity Ability.** When the roles that define us — parent, spouse, employer, employee, athlete, homeowner — come to an end, we have to adapt our sense of self accordingly.

Some people relocate after a divorce to create an entirely new social life with no connection to the one they left behind. They then start considering themselves as independent, rather than one-half of a former couple.

Many jobless people find ways to avoid defining themselves as unemployed. Instead, they create a new identity, like student, community leader, church elder, aspiring artist or entrepreneur.

2. **Selecting Ability.** Making informed choices for our circumstances, even as those circumstances change, is essential to

navigating uncharted territory. Let me give you two examples of people I know:

Roger is a 62-year-old business owner in Stamford, Connecticut, whose primary focus had been work. After his cancer was diagnosed, he was suddenly faced with choices he'd never considered. Who would run his company when he was in treatment? Should he sell the business, and if so, would it be wiser for him to stay on as an executive or stop working altogether?

Then there's Steve, a 59-year-old from Seattle who had a serious bike accident. He found himself needing to decide how to spend his leisure time if he couldn't ever ride again.

Both men sought the counsel of friends (and, in Roger's case, professional advisers) who knew them well and would speak frankly enough to help them remain realistic as they sorted through their options.

3. Meaning-Finding Ability. Managing disruptions and putting them in perspective is a process that can take years. In that time, you must decide how to contextualize the events that are turning your life upside-down and find ways to add meaning to the years you have left.

If you lose a job, do you look at the experience as a failure or a stepping stone to a better position? If a spouse leaves you for a trophy wife or a trust-fund husband, have you been dumped or liberated from a crummy marriage?

Making your life meaningful is especially important as you work through the grieving process — whether you've lost a job, a home, a significant other or something else important to you.

So learn a new skill, make new friends, or plan a massive project, like remodeling your house. Since the interruption can't be undone, it's up to you to recognize that the event has led to a new time in your life that you can embrace and, at least in part, control.

4. Community Ability. One way to manage an interruption is to use it as a launching pad for new activities that challenge and nourish you while also helping others.

Join local organizations, volunteer and stay involved. You'll meet people with similar interests and will be able to contribute your expertise in a way that keeps you intellectually stimulated, socially connected and useful.

5. Financial Reality-Check Ability. Regardless of your best-laid plans, after losing your job or money in an investment, you may have to embark on a new career or find another means of income generation to sustain a reasonable lifestyle as you age.

Fortunately, a new job can bring you unexpected advantages (structure, new friends, fun) in addition to a paycheck. Some companies also provide attractive benefits, like health insurance and paid vacations for employees who work at least 25 hours a week.

Whether or not you're going to work after the age you thought you'd retire, it's a good idea to take a personal finance management course or work with a certified financial planner. Either can help you determine the most suitable savings plan, an appropriate asset allocation for your portfolio and retirement income projections.

Expect the Unexpected

Boomers must face the fact that their decisions, however carefully made, won't *stay* made. Interruptions and redirections are inevitable. Many, if not most, of your choices after 50 will be short-term, rather than long-term.

This means making constant reassessments and adjustments. But take Ability No. 3 to heart: The unexpected will also give you opportunities for renewal that weren't on your radar earlier in your life.

THE JOYS OF NEW FRIENDS

5 ways to keep expanding your social network after age 50

By Linda Bernstein

Linda Bernstein has written hundreds of articles for dozens of magazines and newspapers, writes the blog 'GenerationBsquared' and teaches social media at the Columbia University School of Journalism.

I used to think that by the time your kids flew the nest, major opportunities for meeting new people you really like winged their way out the window as well. I expected that by the time I hit 50, I'd be singing about old acquaintances all the time, not just humming a nostalgic *auld lang syne* chorus on New Year's Eve.

Sure colleges had "parent" committees, but rarely were there face-to-face meetings, given that those parents were flung all over the country. And the only "new" people in the professional arena tended to be, well, more my kids' age than my own.

Experts seem to propound this worldview. In the recent New York Times article "Friends of a Certain Age: Why Is It Hard to Make Friends Over 30?" Laura L. Carstensen, director of the Stanford Center of Longevity in California, argued that as people move toward midlife, they interact with fewer people. Hence, they make fewer friends.

Friends Keep Popping Up All Over

Well, Dr. Carstensen, here I am, old enough that people offer me their seat on the bus — and *I'm meeting people I like all over the place.* My social life is jacked up. Really. The other day my friend Yona came over for lunch. I know Yona through Diane, another recent friend I met through my friend Susan, who was once my boss. This morning Diane told me a silly joke that gave me a laugh exactly when I needed one. Yona recently offered needed emotional support when I made a "career" decision that some would have dubbed "unwise" but I felt relieved me of an unwanted burden. As the song says, "That's what friends are for" — they make you laugh, and they have your back.

Then there's my relatively new friend Amy. I sat next to her at a conference a year and a half ago, and she immediately started introducing me to everyone she knew there (a lot more people than I did), included me in her lunch plans, and has become a generous colleague and one of the people I love spending time with. The thing about Amy is that she's not quite young enough to be my daughter, but almost. (If, like Loretta Lynn, I had been married off as a teen, she would be.)

Sure, there's a bit of a generation gap between us: She has school-age kids, and mine are solidly in their 20s. But my "grandma" and "mom" poles seem to be demagnetized when she tells stories about her boys. I am amused or bemused — a *friend* response. When I worry out loud about my young adult offspring, she doesn't overempathize with them; it's me she relates to and cares about.

This is another surprise: New friends can be quite younger — or older — than I am. When you're 30, a 10-year age difference seems a chasm. It is, after all, one-third of your life. Now that I'm over 50, 40 seems not so far back; 65 not so far ahead. Ann, whom I met running around the reservoir in New York's Central Park, has grandchildren not so much younger than my kids, but she can run at my pace *and* keep up a conversation, largely recounting the previous night's comedic monologues. (Which means I have developed the capacity to laugh and run at the same time.)

These new friends aren't only of the female persuasion — though I believe that if you're married and a new male friend isn't part of a "friendship couple," it may be harder for the two of you to hang out. Yet I can spend hours on Skype with Maxwell, who lives on the West Coast, without making my husband jealous because (a) Maxwell is all of 40, married to a dynamite woman and clearly not interested in me in "that way," and (b) we talk about things like html code and subjects way too tech-geeky to enthrall the philosophy professor I married.

When Maxwell was in town recently and we met for a drink, my husband begged off, knowing he would be bored, bored, bored and confident that nothing would happen IRL.

Five Ways to Make New Friends

"All well and good, Linda," you might be thinking, "but just how do you bring people into your life when, as the experts point out, your opportunities for social interactions are shrinking?"

Answer: Just cast your net—the wider the better. Here's how I found new friends. And I should mention that I'm actually pretty shy, not a natural extrovert, so you can't use that as an excuse.

1. **Take classes.** I am the type who *looovvvees* school. Still, continuing education classes aren't quite "school" for those who didn't like the classroom setting growing up. Mostly you sit around with other adults learning something interesting. You don't have to do homework unless you want to. (But that's the great thing: You'll probably want to).

If there are any colleges or university extensions near you, do a Google search to see what's on offer. Community centers, Ys and religious institutions also frequently host discussion groups and courses. Another place with new friendship possibilities, and don't laugh: Weight Watchers meetings. In person. (Yes, those still happen.) Or spend a day with Habitat for Humanity or another volunteer organization. You'll be exchanging phone numbers by cocktail hour.

2. Join Facebook and LinkedIn. I know: You already did. But are you using them to the max? Facebook is where you can find friends from high school and college with whom you've lost touch. Then, through comments, you meet *their* friends, whom you soon find yourself conversing. I have become friends, and now met in real life, the mother of a young woman about my daughter's age whom I met through work and who "friended" me on Facebook.

Twitter is a wonderful place to discover people you'd never meet otherwise (and sometimes probably will never see face-to-face because they live in, say, New Zealand).

A great thing that has come out of all these online networks is what Twitter folks call the "Tweet Up," but more generally could be simply dubbed a "get-together." People who live nearby but have so far only met online plan a get-together for coffee or a drink. Many times you'll find yourself trying to pin many new faces to names. Other times it's just you and one other person grabbing a cup of coffee. Once you're face-to-face with an online friend, I've found, if you take a shine to each other, you'll start conversing through email and even take it to the phone. If not too much travel is involved, you'll find yourself seeing your new friends regularly.

What can be really fun is literally going the extra mile. A whole bunch of people I know online who live in the Southwest are converging on Phoenix next Saturday .... just *because*. Oh, and when you get social, you'll also get to know friends-of-friends, which is more than a Facebook privacy setting. It's in-real-life people added to your non-virtual social life.

3. Work out at the gym. True, it's not easy having a conversation while you're puffing away on the treadmill or swinging those kettle balls. But what I've found is that there are certain people you see time after time, especially if you take classes. First you start smiling at each other, then you say hi. Finally you have a real conversation in the locker room. Next thing you know, you're grabbing a post-workout coffee with your new gym buddy.

4. **Rediscover old friends.** Not just online, either. There's a woman who lives nearby whom I have kinda-sorta known for years. We were both active in our kids' PTA and spent time together back then. But you know how things go. The kids grew up, and our contacts dwindled to saying "hi" at the supermarket.

Last summer we ran into each other on the block, and she suggested, totally impromptu, that I come and hang in her backyard. We sat around for hours — first bonding over an intense discussion of cleaning products. From there we went on to our kids, our husbands, Broadway shows and, finally, our hopes and dreams. We simply and magically clicked.

Not too long ago I also connected with a woman I knew in college but we had totally lost touch. While talking at a party we discovered we've lived almost parallel lives since graduation. We know the same people, live close by, have children the same age. We even have the same make and model piano! To my good fortune, this re-acquaintance has become a good friend.

I remember having the thought when I was about 18 that as you got older, the people you met would be more interesting because they'd have so many more stories (i.e., experiences) to share. This indeed has proved true. Also, now that we're more comfortable in our own skins and past the age when we feel the need to impress, bonding comes more naturally. We might have more baggage, but it's easier to unpack.

5. **Participate in Meet Ups.** Just Google it. All over the world professional groups schedule meetings for casual conversation and networking. Sometimes a member gives a presentation; other times it's just drinks. Either way, discard your cloak-of-shyness and get out there. I know people who have garnered clients and secured job interviews at these kinds of gatherings. I recently found someone

who told me that she'd look into some little quirky problems I'm having with my website — for free. Also Google "BNI" (Business Networking International) to find a nearby group (which you'll have to apply to join) or "Professional Networks."

Live Long and Prosper

Having great people to hang out with isn't the only benefit to making friends as we get older. Social interactions actually help us live longer, say Brigham Young University professors Julianne Holt-Lunstad and Timothy Smith. "When someone is connected to a group and feels responsibility for other people, that sense of purpose and meaning translates to taking better care of themselves and taking fewer risks," Holt-Lunstad explained. Watching out for our own well-being adds years to our lives.

This research and the joy my new friends bring reminds me of a camp song I learned long ago: "Make new friends, but keep the old. One is silver and the other gold." Except what I'm finding is that new friends *and* old friends are both gold.

WHY I WENT BACK TO COLLEGE

The critical lessons I learned, and what you need to know if you return to school

By John Stark

John Stark is the former articles editor of Next Avenue. He has held top writing and editing positions at such magazines as Cooks' Illustrated, Body + Soul and People. For 14 years, he was a feature writer and movie critic at the San Francisco Examiner/Chronicle.

A few years ago, I went back to college to pursue a master's degree in journalism — at the age of 60. Given my 40 years of experience as a writer and editor at newspapers and magazines, you might ask why I bothered.

The answer is simple: With jobs in print media going the way of polar ice caps, I figured if things got too bad I could turn to teaching. I'd already taught a once-a-week magazine course at Emmanuel College in Boston, but I would need a master's to join the faculty. That's true at most universities and colleges, regardless of your work experience.

I was determined to achieve this goal, even if it would take a few years because I couldn't afford to quit working and become a full-time student. No doubt the Great and Powerful Oz would have told me to forget it — that as a seasoned journalist, I already knew everything I needed to know. But like the Tin Woodsman, I wanted that diploma to confirm it.

And the truth is, I didn't know everything. I hadn't managed to keep up with the media's changing technology. I had plenty to learn.

Overcoming the Initial Fear

I couldn't have picked a scarier time to go back to school. When I applied to Boston University's School of Communications, the economy was at its worst point in decades. Going into debt in the midst of a recession seemed crazy.

Yet that wasn't my biggest fear about returning to school at 60. What made me apprehensive was my age. How would I explain my presence?

It wasn't easy, especially since I was the only older student in any of the eight classes I took. Whenever I walked into a new class on the first day of the semester, I felt self-conscious. I sensed all those young eyes staring at me. It felt as though I could read my classmates' thoughts: Who was I? The professor? Somebody's dad?

But that was just my paranoia. The students didn't regard me as someone 35 years their senior. In fact, my age never came up. I think that's because to young people, everyone past a certain age falls into the same category. You could be 40 or 90 for all they know. For my Intro to Media course, I wrote a blog post titled "Going Like Sixty." A female student whose computer was next to mine asked what I meant by that. When I told her my age, she let out an incredulous shriek: "No way, man! No way!"

Here's a vital tip: If you're taking a course that requires technical know-how, and that's not your strong point, sit close to the T.A. Trust me, it'll help. Take him or her to lunch.

Having sweated through my share of technical screw-ups, I found in the end that my ineptness didn't really matter. I scored an "A" in every new media project I did. The high marks came from my years of work experience. My slide presentations always had a narrative. For a class final, I had to create a Web page that incorporated text, slides, maps, video, interviews and photos. Although I struggled with the technology while putting it together, I knew how to package and focus a story. Contrast that with one of my young classmates, who titled her final project "About Me."

Know When to Shut Up

To get the master's degree, I had to complete some required writing courses. In a way, they were the hardest for me, because they required diplomacy — not with my fellow students, but with the professors. I'm not boasting when I say I know more about writing for newspapers and magazines than an inexperienced 30-year-old (who just happens to have a master's degree). Too many times I found myself contradicting a professor's advice, often using examples, like "When I was at People magazine. . ."

After I had hogged the spotlight once too often, a professor told me after class that I needn't come anymore — she'd just give me the "A."

Still, there were times when I couldn't resist being a smart-ass. I had earned that right. I remember attending a slide show given by a young photography professor. With each iconic image, he'd ask for our impressions.

Although I was quite familiar with the images, I kept my mouth shut — until he showed an Ansel Adams photograph of Yosemite's Half Dome. "How do you think he captured the light?" the professor wanted to know.

I raised my hand.

"If you sit someplace long enough you'll eventually get what you want," I told him.

"And what's that supposed to mean?" the professor asked.

"I'm just saying what Ansel Adams told me when I asked him that question."

The Best Decision

As it turned out, going back to school was the best thing I could have done in a recession. It got me out of the house. Learning to do creative projects with new tools helped take my mind off my shrinking freelance career. Even though times were tough, I was having fun.

Spending time around young people kept me young. Their energy was infectious, and they liked being with me. They were enraptured by my stories about the famous people I'd interviewed, even though they'd never heard of most of them. When we had to pair up for a class project, I was always the first chosen.

And don't get me wrong: I had some great professors, too. Thanks to them, my writing and teaching skills improved. One feature writing professor would analyze our stories by drawing diagrams of them on the blackboard. By creating a skeletal structure, we could see how the story flowed, and if all the components of a good story were there. In my teaching at Emmanuel College, I adapted that visual model. When I signed up for a writing workshop class at Boston University, I wondered how I could bear hearing my stories analyzed by 20-somethings. It was humbling when it turned out their criticisms were pretty astute. If they didn't understand something I wrote, chances are a lot of readers wouldn't either.

Although the technology did intimidate me at first, I did catch on. After a while, you begin to see patterns in how the various programs and systems work. I used the yellow "Dummies" books (*HTML for Dummies*, *Web Design for Dummies*, etc.) as my Cliff Notes. Because technology is always changing, much of what I learned a few years ago is already outdated. But that doesn't matter; what matters is knowing I can adapt. That's a great lesson.

At my age, I have lived enough years to know that things usually work out. Recessions come and recessions go. One of the benefits of getting older is that you finally realize what's important, and it's not always money.

Had I not gone back to school, I would not have had the confidence or skills to apply for a job editing articles on a website. That's the job I have now.

For this recent college grad, the future looks rosy!

How to Find Time and Money to Go Back to School

Here are some of the ways that I made it happen:

* Grad school can cost up to $5,000 a class — it does at B.U. Because I wasn't studying full time, I didn't qualify for student loans. One way I cut costs was to take summer classes. Although they're typically three hours a day, five days a week, they're half price at many schools. Because most students are away in the summer, classes are smaller and more fun. I took a food writing class that had only five students. We elected to hold class one night each week at a different ethnic restaurant.

* As for finding time, again think summer classes. I always took two courses, one starting in June and the other in August. Night classes are another good option if your time is limited, since they're usually held just one night a week. I took one every semester. (Online courses are, of course, another great option for the returning older student. At the time, Boston University's journalism program didn't offer them.)

* Because of my work experience, I was able to get several required classes waived. Colleges want your money. Don't hesitate to bargain.

* Each semester I was able to get an independent study course. For one of these classes I spent four months writing a paper about the Abolitionists of Boston. I didn't have to go to class, just arrange to meet every few weeks with the professor.

THE SURPRISING BENEFITS OF WORKING BACKWARD

Coming at problems from novel perspectives causes the brain to function differently, often yielding unexpected results

By Akiko Busch

Akiko Busch writes about design, culture and the natural world for a variety of publications. Her most recent book, 'The Incidental Steward: Reflections on Citizen Science,' was published by Yale University Press in April 2013.

For a number of weeks this past spring, every time my friend Jane and I would take our regular walk alongside a pond and creek, a bald eagle would swerve in our direction, almost as though to greet us.

Eagles are not new here in New York's Hudson Valley region and their increasing presence speaks to a species restoration project that began 30 years ago. Yet even if it is not uncommon to see this sentinel bird, it is always a privilege to spot one.

What I noticed about *this* eagle, *this* spring, was that it almost always took the exact same flight path. This led me to believe it was nesting in a tall tree near the pond. Weeks of careful observation led nowhere. The nest was not in the towering oak, nor was it in a sycamore tree with a pronounced notch in its upper branches.

Finally one afternoon, in utter frustration, we walked the path backward, looking at the treetops over the pond from a reverse perspective. And there, at last, in the upper limbs of a white pine, we detected the huge, ramshackle bowl of twigs, sticks and branches.

Crazy Wisdom

The exercise, and its reward, put me in mind of how coming at things backward, awkwardly and in uncertain steps can lead to unanticipated and astonishing breakthroughs, and how discoveries can be made at this intersection of the comedic and the sublime.

Folklore suggests that 100 steps backward are as good as 1,000 steps forward. The Lakota Indians honor the "crazy wisdom" of the contrarian Heyoka jokester/sage, who does things like speak in reverse sentences and ride his horse backward.

The value of this tactic isn't just the stuff of folk wisdom and unexpected discoveries. Dutch neuroscientists were curious whether different mental processes are employed when we are walking toward something or away from it. Their study, published in Psychological Science in May 2009, found that subjects who walked even a few steps backward were far more focused and attentive than those who didn't.

The trickster's oppositional approach can work for me as a writer. From time to time when I get stuck on an article or essay, I'll flip the order of the argument, beginning with the conclusion and ending with the introduction. While it's not a structure I am likely to keep, it is an efficient way to reconsider what I'm trying to say.

If it's a profile, bringing a quote from the subject's later years up to the front of the piece may shake up the chronology of the story, but it gives context to what is to come. This isn't exactly the same as walking backward, but it is another mode of stirring up the conventional order of things and finding a fresh, and perhaps stronger, perspective.

Getting Ahead by Moving Backward

Christine Weber, a clinical neuropsychologist in Seaford, N.Y., agrees that reversing the order of one's approach has its benefits.

"This forces the brain to think in a different way — it's a rewiring and changes the focus," she says. "The brain is almost always more active when it comes to novel stimuli and information. A new task makes a new connection in the brain because it has more to process. "When you do something you are unaccustomed to, the signals are different," Weber adds. "This speaks to a plasticity in the brain. And novel things require more cognitive energy; they are not ingrained. As in walking backward — you are not used to it. It requires extra effort."

I suspect this reverse process is not just an exercise of the mind but one of the spirit as well. Paulus Berensohn is an acclaimed ceramist, teacher and writer whose pots and words alike are vessels for reflection. When he was invited to be an artist-in-residence at Haystack Mountain School of Crafts in Deer Isle, Maine, in 1987, he declined the offer, but asked if he could come help prepare food.

In his evocative meditation "Whatever We Touch Is Touching Us," he writes, "I thought I would be more comfortable, perhaps make a more easeful relationship with the students, faculty and staff if I came in through the back door, so to speak. ... So I worked in the kitchen."

Berensohn reflected on how preparing meals, sometimes in silence, was a novel way to enter the community. "It was a new experience for me, this serving of the soup," he said. "At first I was just ... standing there ladling, offering, making contact. Simply serving soup, a little dance, a little communion. This bowl is for you, and this one? It's for you!" A strong, continuing presence at Haystack for decades to come, Berensohn and his kitchen labors revealed to the entire group how the authority of a teacher from time to time depends on a willing and gracious subservience, whether as servant or student.

Surely this is the paradox. The older we get, the more likely we are to understand the intelligent, appropriate, linear progression to attain the things we want and need. Life's experience has taught us to appreciate rationality, consistency, the common-sense, one-step-forward-at-a-time approach to achieving goals, whether they have to do with professional goals, retirement accounts or something else entirely.

Yet at the same time, it also becomes easier to understand that inverting the process has its value too. Incongruity, surprise and the utterly unexpected angle offer their own lessons. Discovering the eagle's nest, whether it is literal or figurative, can be the result of reversal as much as one of advance.

WHY YOU'LL LIVE LONGER IF YOU TAKE MUSIC LESSONS

Studies show all kinds of mental and physical perks when you pick up an instrument

By Matthew Solan

Matthew Solan is a veteran writer and editor who has contributed to numerous publications and websites, including Men's Health, Runner's World, Harvard Men's Health Watch, Yoga Journal and Vegetarian Times.

My first instrument was a used bass guitar I bought in high school for $70 at Florida Discount Music in Melbourne, where I grew up. I never took any lessons. Instead, I spent hours next to my turntable and tried to mimic the riffs from U2, The Who and Cream. (My attempt at "Sunshine of Your Love" lasted about 10 minutes).

The bass proved an entertaining hobby, yet by the time I got to college it was demoted to garage sale status, and ever since my music-making ability has consisted of downloading songs from iTunes.

But now is the best time to find that beat again.

As we age, our cognitive skills weaken. It's the adage: Use it or lose it. Learning a musical instrument can be one of the best workouts for your mind, and as research has revealed, it also can soothe an aging body and even rekindle the soul.

Just look at what making music can do:

Better Memory and Hearing

A 2011 study from Northwestern University looked at musicians aged 45 to 65 and found that their auditory memory and ability to hear speech in noisy environments were better than those of non-musicians of the same age.

The reason, says Nina Kraus, director of the Auditory Neuroscience Laboratory at Northwestern, is that music training "fine tunes" the nervous system. She equates the effect to how painters are attuned to the visual aspects of their craft. They are laser-focused on the slightest differences in paint texture, the lines of a subject's face, and how light affects a setting. This same reaction can occur when music is the main point of reference.

"When the material you work with is sound, then it makes sense that your ability to take it in, remember it, and relate to it should be sharpened," Kraus says.

Better Physical Health

Research from the Music Making and Wellness project — a five-year study that involved music experts from universities and colleges across the country — shows that the level of human growth hormone, or HGH, increased 90 percent in seniors who were given keyboard lessons. HGH is an essential chemical that helps slow many aging conditions, like osteoporosis, loss of muscle mass, and aches and pains. HGH decreases with age – by as much as 50 percent in people older than 40.

Better Mental Health

It has been well documented that listening to music relaxes the mind, reduces anxiety, and alleviates depression. And it doesn't matter if those soothing and inspiring tunes come from an iPod or live from a Steinway. This effect can even be more satisfying and powerful if the music emanates from you. "Hearing music by pushing a piano key or strumming a guitar creates an instant gratification," says Jennifer Diedrich, a piano and violin instructor with Suzuki Strings in St. Petersburg, Florida. "There is that rush where you say to yourself, 'Hey, I made those sounds!'"

Research led by Dr. Barry Bittman of the Mind-Body Wellness Center in Meadville, Pennsylvania, found that playing a musical instrument reduces stress more than other traditional relaxing activities, like reading a newspaper or magazine.

Getting Started on an Instrument

Even when adults have the required dedication to learn an instrument, it is important to also tap into their child-mind, Diedrich says. "Many adults are analytical — they want the music to be perfect and they miss the joy of just making music," she says. "If kids mess up they just plow through it. They act first and think later, and adults should follow that lead and always remember that making music should be enjoyable."

You can't learn without a good teacher. When choosing an instructor, Diedrich says, make sure he or she complements your goals and interest. One obvious example: If you want to play jazz piano, don't hire someone who specializes in classical. If possible ask to observe a teacher to get a feel for chemistry and his or her approach to teaching.

Finding the Ideal Instrument

What's the best instrument to play? The one you are excited to learn. After all, it will take practice and persistence to improve and perhaps master, so you don't want to embrace something you might regret after a few months. (So maybe think twice about the five-piece drum set.)

Diedrich says the piano and acoustic guitar are both ideal as they often require minimal movements to produce pleasing sounds. More complex instruments like, say, the violin have so many specific physical requirements — how to handle the bow and where to place your fingers — that you may end up focusing too much on technique rather than the music.

But once you decide you want to learn, locating the instrument that will be your musical soul mate should come easily.

I have already found mine. It hangs in the window of a St. Petersburg guitar shop, which is run by two guys who I am sure were roadies for Lynyrd Skynyrd. It's a bitchin' Fender Precision Bass. On sale. All black and shiny and majestic.

I think it's time I give "Sunshine" another try.

9 BEST THINGS ABOUT BEING OVER 50

Next Avenue readers share their insights about the many benefits of growing older, including their hard-won wisdom

By Donna Sapolin

Donna Sapolin, the founding Vice President and Editorial Director of Next Avenue, is a multi-platform media consultant, editor and writer who has led many leading magazines and websites and written hundreds of articles.

I've been poring over the many wise and intriguing reactions to Next Avenue articles, blog posts and discussion questions. Our readers have many wonderful things to say about the process of getting older and how they feel about where they are in the second stage of adult life. The perspectives, passions and pursuits they've shared with us confirm nine core benefits to being over 50.

1. **We can opt for a positive attitude.** "Old age is not for sissies," says reader Meriel Collins, 66, in response to this article about common yet often unrecognized difficulties of aging. "It's for the gutsy, the flexible, those who are still *interested* in having a quality life.

"I am grateful for life and the love of family and good friends," she adds. "Just say 'thank you' for the good things, acknowledge what you have learned from the not-so-good and embrace the possibilities the future holds. Find a reason to get up every morning; find something to look forward to — that's what keeps life interesting."

Lorie Eber agrees. "There are good and bad things about every phase of life," she writes. "Just go with glass half-full — you only get one chance, so you might as well choose to be happy!" That point is echoed by Susan McMinn Robins. "Attitude makes the biggest difference," she says, "and not being afraid to reinvent yourself or try new things."

2. **Adventure awaits us — now's the time to be bold.** "I work on a college campus and love the hustle and bustle of the students, plus the myriad exhibits, performances, etc., at a reasonable price," Barbara Shramo says. "I'll be 70 this year and can't believe it. Keep learning and moving."

That's exactly what Ginnis Equality does all year long, thanks to her assorted, often vigorous hobbies. "When I am not biking, I may be kayaking, which is great on hot summer days," she writes. "I go cross-country skiing all winter, heading to groomed trails so I can 'skate' ski, like you see in the Olympics, only tremendously slower. I also love cooking nutritious food, playing Scottish fiddle, and writing poetry."

Helga von Harsdorf-Johnson's pending sense of adventure is sparked by family. "My daughter and granddaughter live in Rome and intend to stay there," she notes. "I am thinking of going there when I fully retire, it is a bit scary too since I will be old and have lived in the Washington area since 1974 ... new beginnings ... scary!"

3. **We've got more wisdom and fewer regrets.** "Give up regrets," Pia Louise advises. "I almost destroyed myself over things I cannot change. ... I've reinvented myself: I moved to a thumpin', bumpin' city so vibrant and alive it's contagious.

"I do not think on the past anymore," she says. "I have a whole new joie de vivre thing goin' on. I'm so present to my life — I went from zero to 10. It took some time, but I could not be happier. My advice: Get up, keep goin'. You've come this far, be who you dream you want to be! Do it!"

4. There's greater independence — and so many options!
"I feel a sense of freedom and possibility not experienced maybe since I graduated high school!" Syndee Leigh says. "Kids doing well in their young adult lives have allowed me the opportunity to run a bit amok and feel quite young again. I may look like crap, but I am *so* past it. This may be my favorite phase!"

"I see my life unfolding with infinite possibilities," Nancy Robinson writes. "I treasure the adventures and look forward to things that have not happened yet. I also love to laugh. More and more, I can laugh at myself. Some of the things I do seem pretty funny to me. What a wonderful time to be alive. I never knew getting older would be so much fun!"

Gaye Saucier Farris knows the exact same feeling. "I found a new joy," she says, "because I have the freedom of time to finally do what I want to do, when I want to do it: volunteer at my granddaughter's school and the community theater; join the theater guild and a book club of extraordinary women; and even celebrate with a 'girls night out' group from my tiny neighborhood that is full of the friendliest people I have ever known. After years of my editing science research, out of the blue came a commission to edit a novel."

5. Life is less selfish these days. "We can focus on our inner selves, on who we really are," Sandy Interrante eloquently states. "In the later stages of life, it's a gift if we can focus on others with kindness and compassion when they need it. To be able to really listen to others will leave a far greater imprint than trying to look younger. A kind word, a moment of caring, an attempt to help will ripple out into the universe with positive energy that will bring us purpose and self-respect in our final years."

6. There's joy to be found in all kinds of simple things.
Jacqueline Burke Howard's daily To Do list doesn't come across as a litany of chores. "I paint, walk my dog, read lots and do more cooking, church work and activities," she reports. "I notice the beauty of nature more too. God is good. I can be as happy as I want to be."

Reading is a great passion for many Next Avenue visitors and they are immersing themselves more deeply now than ever before. "I'm an avid reader — real books, not e-books," Leslie Blackston Favors says. "I read every day. My favorite topics are finance, health and fitness, science and cooking."

Marcie A. Rosenzweig, along with many other Next Avenue readers, counts gardening among her hobbies: "I'm a dirt addict so I garden as much as my body will let me," she says. "I used to have an organic vegetable farm, so the garden keeps my sanity."

7. We're curious about the future and determined to keep moving forward. Tm Willingham speaks to "the value of having the age and maturity to be able to self-assess without self-consciousness, and decide if I like what I see in the mirror," she says. "I tend to embrace change — I just had a conversation with someone about this. I like seeing what's around the next corner, learning a new skill, trying something I've never tried before, and improving myself by finding a way to overcome what I might consider a personal shortcoming. Every time I succeed at something new, I feel empowered to try something else. And when I don't succeed, I'm mature enough to know it's only a temporary setback, not a life sentence."

8. We can choose to move more lightly through the world. Bill Lavery details his plan to shed all but the essentials as he takes up residence in a new locale each year. "Downtown Kansas City, midtown Manhattan, Old Town Toronto. They start out foreign, but quickly become domestic. Plans for future locations include Montreal, Belgium, and Alsace. ... We keep moving lighter and lighter and picking up nothing that can't be left behind to Goodwill. We only rent fully furnished apartments and don't keep cars, renting those for special needs only. People say that they would like to get to their college weight. My goal is to get back down to my college possessions."

9. We can focus on expressing love in all kinds of ways. Karen Irving is quick to acknowledge one of the keys to showing care and concern. "Definitely hugs," she says, "but even more important is listening to the person — really listening, not just nodding at the appropriate moments — and asking questions that show I want to understand what they're talking about.

"I'm also a fan of the heartfelt compliment," she adds. "I don't offer them lightly, so when I tell my kids I'm proud of something they've done, they know I really mean it."

Macia Riis Tyrol deals with her loved ones in a similar way. She spends time with them "doing what they love to do," she says. "I keep connected and present in their lives with phone calls, texts and emails. Most importantly, I tell them they matter, that I am here for them and I believe in them."

HOW TO REALLY FORGIVE SOMEONE

A psychologist, a bishop and a filmmaker discuss why we need not forgive and forget but should forgive and remember

By Akiko Busch

Akiko Busch writes about design, culture and the natural world for a variety of publications. Her most recent book, 'The Incidental Steward: Reflections on Citizen Science,' was published by Yale University Press in April 2013.

Forgiveness is a complicated subject, as we were recently reminded when two disgraced New York politicians announced their campaigns. Former governor Eliot Spitzer, running for state comptroller, asked voters to forgive his past penchant for prostitutes, while shamed ex-Congressman Anthony Weiner continued to plead with constituents to overlook his lewd photos, sexting and subsequent lies.

These comeback endeavors were met with mixed feelings, ranging from skepticism to outrage to an attitude of forgive and forget.

It is the latter reaction that puzzles me most.

Why is forgiveness so often linked with forgetting? Is it some reflexive cheek-turning that Christians believe is a virtue? Does it have to do with some societal instinct for denial? Or is it our accelerated culture and 24/7 news cycle that force us to move on at all costs?

I would make an argument for forgiving and *remembering.*

Recast this way, the emphasis shifts from holding a grudge or hanging on to slights to using the ability we develop to confront transgression. It also entails considering the full complement of experience, actions and words that might explain the motives behind an act then fully absorbing its meaning. Only then can one find a way to move on.

Learning to Reframe the Story

Anyone who has raised a child should have this ability, since acceptance is part of a parent's job description. It can be relatively easy to absolve a broken platter, muddy floor or spilled food. But the behavior that may lie behind the act — carelessness, thoughtlessness or selfishness — calls for different measures, whether empathy, discipline or tougher demands.

Unlike with such small childhood offenses, a different manner of accounting comes into play with larger issues that involve betrayal, violation of a public trust, or more profound gestures of hurt, be it a cumulative emotional injury or acts of raw, physical violence. Colin Tipping, the founder of a program he calls Radical Forgiveness, suggests that one important avenue to pardon is storytelling.

"It is a way of bringing all the feelings associated with the content of the story to the surface so they can be seen and confronted," says Tipping. "It is a way of validating one's feelings in the sense that it gives us a context and a justification for having them. It allows us to work through the emotions that do come up, using compassion, empathy, understanding and mercy, all of which we can extend to ourselves as well as others."

We can tell the story to ourselves, Tipping continues, "but it is more powerful if we tell it to someone else, so long as they have the right'listening' for it and can validate it for us and be there with us when the feelings arise. I believe the telling of the story and feeling the feelings fully is essential to the process of healing our fears and expanding into love."

Tipping believes forgiveness begins with relearning the story of the offense — that is, reconsidering it with an understanding of the circumstances from which it came. But that's only the beginning. Eventually, he suggests, one can also become aware of its greater "spiritual purpose." Or at least accept the possibility that such a meaning exists.

I suspect many of us have some familiarity with this process. I witnessed it in a friend who noticed that the anger she felt toward her father — who had abandoned the family when she was a child — diminished when she was in her 30s.

Only after she had faced financial adversity of her own could she empathize with his account of the professional insecurity and financial shame that led him to leave his wife and kids. And she came to believe that her eventual fiscal acumen as an adult was the positive effect of a nearly primal sense of economic vulnerability she had experienced as a child and her desire to overcome it.

The Path to Reconciliation and Redemption

Archbishop Desmond Tutu of South Africa came to understand what a powerful tool storytelling can be as head of his country's Truth and Reconciliation Commission. Its directive: Get the victims and perpetrators of apartheid to confront each other. Its premise: The narrative exchange was the only means by which the country could begin to heal.

Tutu has come to believe that forgiveness emerges from a transformative dialogue between the person hurt and the person inflicting pain. "To forgive is not just to be altruistic," he has said. "It is the best form of self-interest." His words are reprinted on the site for the Forgiveness Project, a U.K.-based international initiative that collects the testimony from crime victims and their perpetrators.

The underlying premise is that when stories are told, reconciliation and redemption can follow.

On the site, we hear about a Canadian woman who has given absolution to her husband's murderer; a Palestinian father who has forgiven the Israeli soldier guilty of shooting his young daughter; a Polish woman who pardons a Nazi doctor who used her for medical research at Auschwitz. Story upon story upon story, they construct a radiant message board for human charity.

Part of how genuine forgiveness works is by taking us outside of ourselves. In the process, it enriches and expands our comprehension and acceptance of human beings and their behavior. "Healing comes through understanding," Tutu says. It comes from listening to stories, assigning them to memory, and retaining them forever. Forgiveness is a spiritual exercise that has to do with many things, but forgetting is not among them.

Overcoming Anger and Desire for Revenge

Helen Whitney, a writer and documentary filmmaker, expands on that theme in the introduction to her book, *Forgiveness: A Time to Love and a Time to Hate*. "Forgiveness is not a question of forgetting the wrong done," she writes. "If you've forgotten what was done, there is nothing to forgive. Forgiveness involves refusing to allow yourself to give in to anger and the desire for revenge."

In her PBS film, *Forgiveness*, Whitney explores the subject in an effort to, as she says, "complicate it." Whether it is a radical activist's efforts to atone for a political murder, Rwandans' efforts to legislate forgiveness for genocide, Germany's efforts toward restitution after the Holocaust, or a family's divided feelings toward a mother who left her children, how we learn to exonerate wrong is a passage of conscience.

Each of these cases demonstrates that forgiveness, whether requested or given, is a matter not of negating, denying or assigning the iniquity to oblivion, but of confronting it and absorbing it fully. And all require an interior discourse.

In the course of that dialogue, when the weight of guilt is lifted from the abuser, so too is the burden of victimhood lifted from the abused. But above all, Whitney says, it takes time. Quick, easy, careless forgiveness can both degrade the power of the offense and diminish the profound and positive force of absolution.

The psychologist, the bishop and the filmmaker have all discovered that the human ability to inflict pain can be matched — and trumped — by a capacity for charity. If this can hold true with acts of extreme hatred, political atrocity and genocide, surely it has application in less extreme circumstances. Whether it is a politician, partner, friend or child, it is possible to extend grace and to grant full and unconditional pardon without denying poor choices, egregious judgment and painful actions.

"Forgiveness can purify memory," Whitney says, quoting Pope John Paul II. That seems to be key. It makes sense, then, to believe that remembering — as opposed to forgetting — is vital to the process of absolution. It requires remembering your own experience, the nature of the offense, the character of the offender. And then, above all, remembering the humanity that binds us together.

HOW TO HIT 'RESTART' AFTER AGE 50

Tips and information from the self-anoited 'blue jeans queen' of reinvention

By Diane Gilman

Diane Gilman is the driving force behind the most successful fashion brand at HSN with her "DG2" line of jeans, tailored to 40-plus women, and the author of 'Good Jeans: 10 Simple Truths about Feeling Great, Staying Sexy & Aging Agelessly.'

You may not know me, but you might be familiar with my jeans. Not to brag, but they're the top-selling item on the Home Shopping Network, and I created them specifically for women over 40.

To some people, the most fascinating aspect of my story is my dramatic success as a fashion designer. But personally, I'm most proud of the fact that today, in my 60s and after a lifetime of struggles, I am finally attaining everything I ever dreamed of — professionally, personally and even romantically.

To call my early life traumatic is a huge understatement. I grew up with a violent, abusive father and a cold, unprotecting mother. But I overcame my demons and have made it my mission to help others to follow their dreams. That's what inspired me to write my first book, *Good Jeans: 10 Simple Truths About Feeling Great, Staying Sexy and Aging Agelessly* —the desire to teach people how they can not only reinvent themselves, but maximize their fulfillment and happiness at any age.

A Real-Life Rags-to-Riches Story

I sometimes describe my childhood as "growing up *Addams Family* in a *Leave It to Beaver* world" — long on abuse, but short on love. I left home as a teenager and never looked back. I made my way in the world with my fashion-design skills, and the things that happened to me along the way read like a romance novel.

In the 1960s, I went from being a small-time "hippie designer" to making outrageous denim costumes for Janis Joplin, Jimi Hendrix and other top rockers. I migrated from California to New York City in the '70s and opened a little boutique. One sunny afternoon my entire inventory was bought out by a single customer: Cher.

A number of years later, struggling to make ends meet, I was working at Bloomingdale's by day and waitressing at Max's Kansas City by night. One day at the store, the fashion director made a surprise appearance and laid a number of demands on us. As I scrambled to respond, I purposefully mentioned that I was also a designer. Kindly, she agreed to see my clothes. I nearly killed myself hand-cutting and sewing a small collection, which I presented to her a month later.

She was so blown away that she summoned the design director at the then-popular Abraham & Straus department store. They gave me $100,000 of orders and even paid to have them fabricated. In 1989 my business peaked and my spring sportswear collection, particularly the cabal blouse, was in the window of every major department store in New York.

For all the glamour of that world, however, I didn't make a lot of money until the mid-'90s, when I was in my late 40s. Tele-retailing giant HSN asked if I would be interested in designing a line just for them and then appear on TV to sell it. I happened to be embroiled in a terrible lawsuit with a Chinese conglomerate that promised to make me rich if I signed away my name to them. I had, and as a result, my business was hamstrung.

Here I was: a designer who'd given away rights to her own name and couldn't legally sell her clothes in stores. And I was hemorrhaging what little money I had in the lawsuit. Even though tele-retailing was a relatively new game (and hardly a career aspiration), I felt I had no choice but to say yes to HSN.

It wasn't smooth sailing out of the gate. Just as I came on air, my soul mate of 18 years, Jim, received a diagnosis of terminal prostate and liver cancer. I was barely 50 when he died; I refer to the next 10 years of my life as my "lost decade." The suffocating grief sent me into a deep depression and I gained 60 pounds. I couldn't focus on my designs and it brought my business to an all-time low.

Somewhere around 57, I finally lost the weight through a serious commitment to exercise and diet. That was great, but then I needed a new wardrobe. The washable silk I sold on TV wasn't right because those designs were meant to hide a mature figure. I wanted to flaunt my new silhouette and get my sexy back.

I tried to think of one fashion item that would exemplify ageless sex appeal. I decided it was a perfect-fitting jean. I shopped everywhere but found only baggy mom-jeans or ridiculously youthful low riders. Appropriate tops were easy to find, but a proper bottom for a body like mine was impossible.

Out of utter frustration, I designed a line of jeans that would flatter my figure. And I knew if this made me happy, it would likely appeal to millions of women. I approached HSN — and they loved it.

Within a year, I owned the marketplace. Now, in 2013, we are projected to sell $120 million worth of DG2 jeans on HSN. For me, the money and recognition are wonderful, of course, but I'm also thrilled that my personal rejuvenation has gone hand-in-hand with my professional one. I didn't realize it was a cardinal rule of reinvention at the time, but I simply used my personal experience and needs to start a niche business. I not only made the brand, I *was* the brand.

And then, magic happened. As impossible as it would have seemed 17 years earlier, I met another wonderful man. I had loved Jim, but the man I warmly call Attila is my true romantic partner. Today, seven years later, we are still madly in love.

How to Hit Your Own Restart Button

Bottom line: You need to believe in yourself and trust in your ability to create your own reality. Here are the three golden rules I've learned along the way for jump-starting the second half of life.

1. **Don't treat your career as "business as usual."** You've paid your dues. Act 2 is born out of your own deep yearnings. Many midlifers become entrepreneurs to avoid battling the corporate job market, where "younger and cheaper is better" is the motto and ageism, sadly, is rampant. I think niche-oriented products that grow out of a personal passion will hook your interest most. I followed my gut, acting on the belief that what worked for me would work for millions of others. While it's important to be practical, you also need to let your heart have a say in your decision-making process.

2. **Throw out the old dating rules.** Midlife romance can be like trying to do the tango without ever taking a lesson. Most of us have had no guidance or role models, so too often we treat Act 2 relationships as if things haven't changed since we were young adults. Yet almost everything has. For starters, we're no longer looking for the father of our future children. We know ourselves and our desires (and intolerances) so much better, plus we have reached a mature understanding that we don't need a mate to feel whole or "legitimate."

While Attila is 14 years my junior, I am not a cougar. (Jim was a decade older than me.) I wasn't seeking a younger man, but that's what my energy pulled in, and it's perfect for me since I have a young spirit. I am experiencing the wildest romance of my lifetime. I believe it finally happened because I worked so hard to keep my heart open to the possibility of love and not close myself off like many midlifers do.

The most important thing — no matter how doubtful, fearful or insecure you are — is to be truthful with yourself. So many of us of a certain age shut ourselves down and convince ourselves that we no longer want or need sex, fun, companionship or romance. We have to release limiting beliefs and decide anew what we do or don't want then map out a path to get there. Don't sit around waiting for love to find you; be proactive. Sign up for an Internet dating site or join a singles adventure travel club or whatever group appeals to you.

3. Get in shape for what's next. You'll need an infusion of energy and self-esteem to spark your reinvention. For me it started with losing as much of that extra weight as possible. As you know, diet or exercise alone aren't enough. You need to make some shifts on both fronts simultaneously. The nice thing is this helps deepen your body-mind connection, which includes learning to listen, feel and react authentically.

When I was 60 pounds heavier, I was always exhausted and sluggish. I had disconnected my mind from my body and bought into the myth that this was just how you feel in middle age. Then I got back into working out and learned that joint-pounding exercises weren't appropriate for me anymore. I did my research and found fusion workouts, a blend of gentle yoga with core- and weight-strengthening moves. These are great ways to build muscle, strength and flexibility, burn fat and increase your self-confidence and self-esteem.

My last piece of advice is the most important. Refocus your reality and reset — not lower — your expectations. When it comes to exercise, don't aim for a rock-solid six-pack or Madonna's arms. Don't confuse a sense of success with a certain number in your bank account or gauge true love by how it *looks*. Relish everything you've learned and accomplished and use those talents to further your development. The more open you are to different possibilities, the more positive results you'll achieve.

WANT TO AGE WELL? LEARN NEW TRICKS, NOT FACTS

A PBS special, 'Hopeful Aging,' explains how we can use the brain's hardwired learning abilities to enhance our lives, even as we grow older

By John Zeisel, Ph.D

John Zeisel, Ph.D., is President of Hearthstone Alzheimer Care and the I'm Still Her Foundation. His latest book is 'I'm Still Here: A Breakthrough Approach to Understanding Someone Living with Alzheimer's.' His television special, 'Hopeful Aging,' aired on PBS stations nationwide in spring 2013.

Many people define aging negatively, as a long downward slope filled with loss, illness and loneliness. But it doesn't have to be that way. It's up to us to decide how, and how well, we want to age.

Where do we find hope? Where do we look for answers to the question of how to create a life worth living for ourselves? Not at the sensational headlines about new drugs, creams, exercise machines and radical diets that can "keep us young." The implication of such reports is that we have to remain young and "fight" aging — as if we had a choice.

A more hopeful place to look is to the growing field of neuroscience, the study of the brain and how it functions, whose work is about to be bolstered by a major, federally driven, decade-long project to map the workings of the brain.

My PBS special, *Hopeful Aging,* begins with an exploration of the brain's crucial role in our lives as we age. We all know that our brain is responsible for our ability to remember, prioritize, solve problems and generally make sense of the world around us. But how can we help it do all those things? What must we understand about the brain to keep it working as well as it can? What's the key?

For humankind to survive, we have always had to figure things out. Our brains are built to feed our curiosity, our urge to discover, uncover and invent — essentially, to be creative. And if we stay creative, and continually learn, we will be helping our brains give us a life worth living as we age.

I don't just mean solving crossword puzzles or playing computer games. Those activities may stimulate our brains, but they only use what we already have in there. What we need to do is to explore new subjects and discover new skills while continuing to nurture old skills.

Think of people you know who used to draw, take photographs, write poetry or dance. In many cases, they stopped their activity because they felt: "What's the use? I will never be as good at these things as I used to."

Hogwash. As we age, we gain insight, vision and wisdom, all of which will serve our creativity well, if we just work up the courage to jump in and try once again to see the world anew.

New Standards

One of the worst things about scientists (and I'm a social scientist myself) is that we develop measurement tools that determine not only how to gauge phenomena but also *which* phenomena to track. We decide what we consider important and relevant. So, for example, we often hear that older people cannot remember things as well as younger people, like random facts, series of numbers and linked word pairs. But is that really what's important as we age? I don't think so.

Just as crucial is our emotional knowledge of how to care for others, support those in need, or find just the right word to express a feeling. Just as important is the knowledge we retain to putt a golf ball or move gracefully with a partner on the dance floor. Just as important is that we never stop being creative or trying to teach others what we know.

Who tests those skills? Who cherishes them? Who makes a priority of identifying our strengths as we age, rather than cataloging our weaknesses and deficits? Not many people. So we need to do it ourselves.

What standards should we set for ourselves to continue to have a life worth living?

Take care of your body and your mind will follow. The more we learn about memory and creativity, the more we discover that basic good health is fundamental to preserving those skills — starting with regular exercise, a healthy diet and deep sleep. That's obvious, perhaps, but these goals are hard for many of us to achieve. They are major lifestyle commitments that most of us don't make, except as briefly kept New Year's resolutions.

Reduce stress through playfulness and meditation. Resting our mind and letting it wander into new and imaginative worlds can reduce stress, limit the effects of chronic inflammation and bolster our immune system. And just think what fun it is to play games with friends and grandchildren.

Embrace creativity regularly. Participation in the arts, especially music and dance, can have a significant effect in warding off dementia. Subscribe to a concert series or get a museum membership. Join a discussion group, take a drawing class at a community center or learn how to tango at a dance school. The possibilities are infinite. All it takes is deciding to do it.

Exercise your abilities and learn new skills. True learning — not just the stimulation of tabletop puzzles — is the final key to hopeful aging. This means taking advantage of the "procedural learning" part of the brain, which does not diminish in capacity. Keep practicing the skills you've mastered by repetition throughout your life, like shooting baskets or drawing a picture, not the stuff you learned through "declarative," or rote, memory, like the name of the 12th president. Rote-learned information is what we forget and can't recall, but our procedural skills remain and can be exercised and enhanced every day as we get older.

Procedural learning — the acquisition of abilities, not facts — is a crucial key to lifelong learning. Identify what's meaningful to you then employ hardwired brain skills like curiosity and creativity — abilities you'll never lose, even if you haven't employed them in a while — to enhance your life, help others and participate in your community. It is one of nature's amazing gifts that even if someone has dementia or Alzheimer's, they can still exercise the brain's deeply hardwired ability to have a life worth living.

ABOUT NEXT AVENUE

America is in the midst of an age boom and with it, an amazing transition. In general, those of us over the age of 50 are expected to live longer than any previous generation.

We're in the process of creating a new life stage that lies somewhere between young adulthood and "old-old" adulthood. This stage doesn't have a name. We call it Adult Part 2. And if you're reading this you're probably smack dab in it.

You're aware that many years of life lie ahead of you and, very likely, you have a different set of expectations for these "bonus years" than you had for earlier adulthood. You sense that you can somehow apply your knowledge and experiences in a meaningful way. Yet you may not know exactly how to achieve this new vision or see all the many possibilities available to you as you navigate the physical, health, work, and financial shifts that inevitably accompany this phase.

Enter **Next Avenue**. We're a group of public television people and journalists who, for the most part, are experiencing the very same things you are. Like you, we see both challenges and opportunities and we recognize that what we could all use right about now is an abundance of reliable information that can help us figure out what's, well, next.

So we aim to deliver that—in a way that's both smart and accessible.

Thanks for walking with us down Next Avenue.

ABOUT DONNA SAPOLIN

As Founding Editor of Next Avenue, Donna Sapolin has been
steeped in the issues and stories of Adult, Part 2. A longtime magazine editor and writer, she curated this collection from writings that
originally appeared on nextavenue.org.

For more Next Avenue e-books, please visit the PBS
Digital Shop!

Made in the USA
San Bernardino, CA
21 March 2015